THIS CANDLEWICK BOOK BELONGS TO:

_____

_____

_____

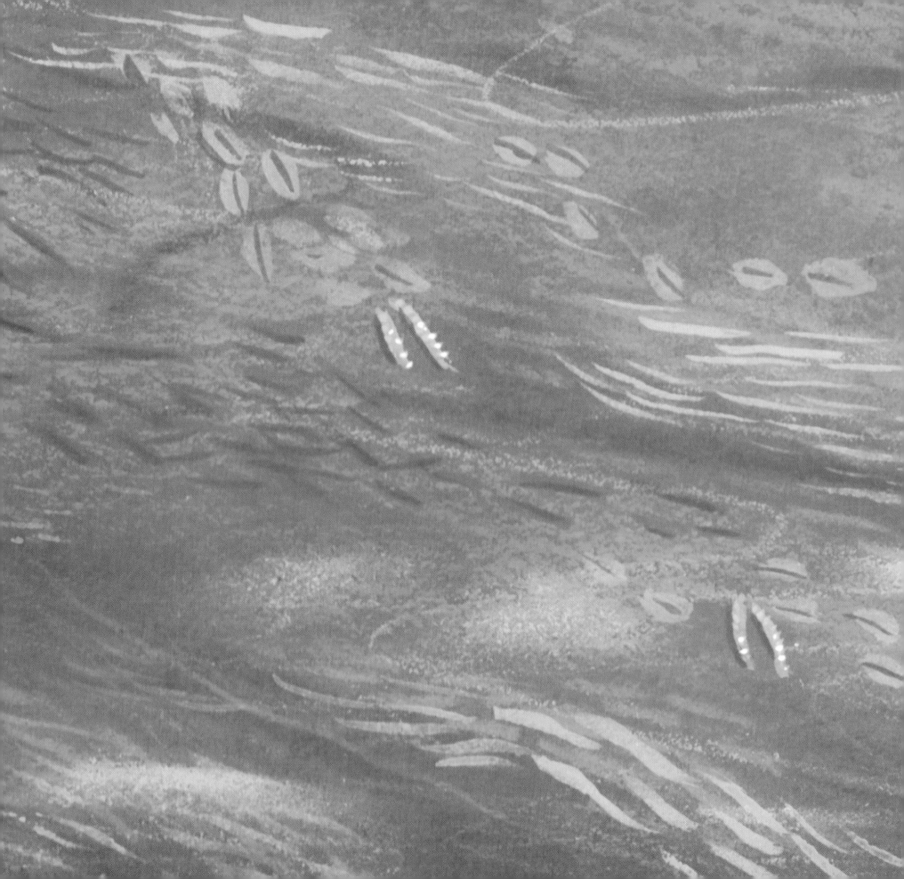

Thousands of rivers help to shape the surface of our planet. They bring water and life to the land and all that use it. Icy-cold racing rivers, slow muddy wide rivers, long rivers, small rivers, rivers underground. Each river is different. Each river makes its own exciting, mysterious journey.

Join us on this one.

To Jean and Anne-Marie, who live on a river
M. H.

To Herman, with thanks
B. W.

Text copyright © 2000 by Meredith Hooper
Illustrations copyright © 2000 by Bee Willey

First U.S. paperback edition 2015

Library of Congress Cataloging-in-Publication Data is available.

Library of Congress Catalog Card Number 99053730

ISBN 978-0-7636-7646-9

19 20 APS 10 9 8 7 6 5

Printed in Humen, Dongguan, China

This book was typeset in Vendome.
The illustrations were done in oil, pastel, acrylic, and pencil.

Candlewick Press
99 Dover Street
Somerville, Massachusetts 02144

visit us at www.candlewick.com

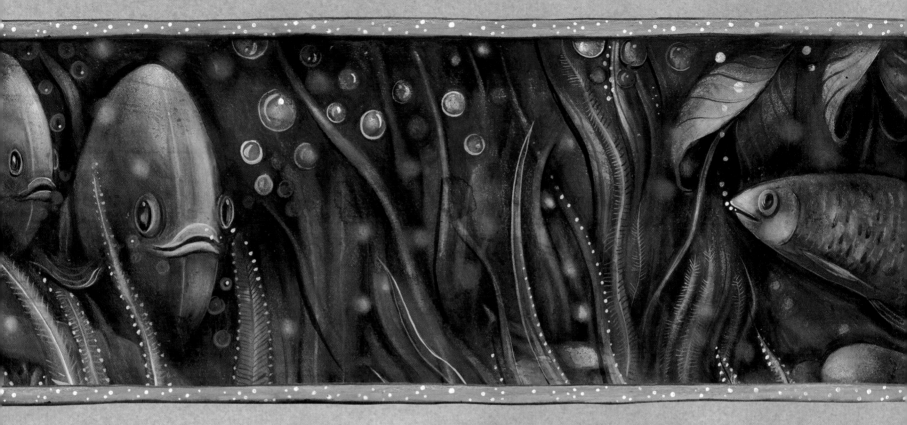

RIVER STORY

Meredith Hooper ❧ illustrated by Bee Willey

CANDLEWICK PRESS

All rivers have a beginning....

High in the mountains

the snow is melting.

Trickles of water are running together,

bubbling through moss,

dripping down ledges,

coming together into a stream.

A small shining stream,

slipping over pebbles,

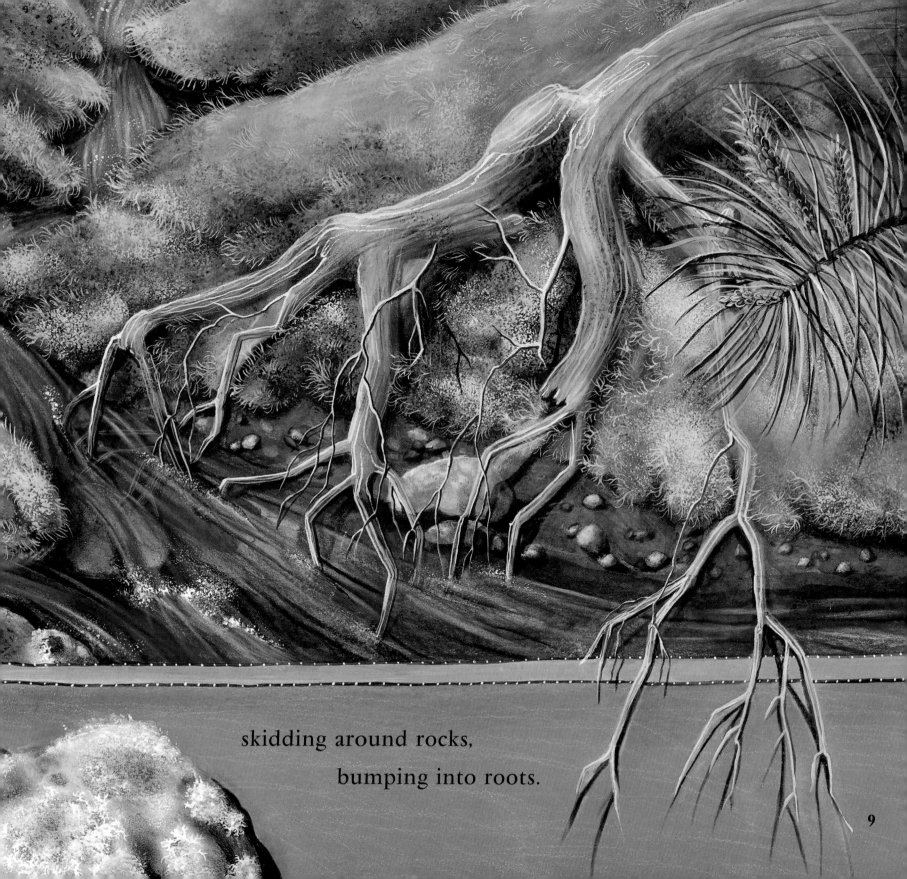

skidding around rocks,

bumping into roots.

9

Fed by a waterfall,

bouncing down boulders.
Fed by another stream,
smaller and faster.

Snowfalls of water,
springfuls of water,
streamfuls of water,
coming together into a river.

The river races

down deep, narrow valleys.

Milky-cold,

rattling-bold,

fast-moving river.

Scooping up earth,

digging out stones,

mining the mountains,

wearing them down.

The river swirls busily
under a bridge.

Stand on the bridge and

look down at the water.

You can't see the bottom.

You can't see how deep.

You can't see the shapes hidden under the surface.

Trunks of old trees, big fish waiting,

little fish darting,

    bottles dropped, treasures lost.

The river is quieter

leaving the mountains.

It winds between meadows,
long strands of waterweed
streaking its surface.

Willow trees lean their leaves
in the water. People row boats,
trailing their fingers.

Cows come drinking,
their sharp hooves sinking
into the sticky-brown river-brown mud.

19

The river grows wider,

and deeper, and stronger.

Fast currents ripple

its silky brown surface.

The water moves silently,

on to the city.

Inside the city
the river is crowded,
jostled by buildings,
hemmed in by roads.

The traffic moves over
and under and around it.
Drains spill their water.
Stray dogs slink by.

And up and down the river go

slow-moving barges
and bright busy ferries,
shiny glass tour boats
and tough little tugs.

The river is slowing,
sliding past mud flats,
looping through marshes,
carrying its load
of earth and leaves,
tin cans and cartons,
and bits of old wood.

24

Where the river reaches
the edge of the land,

waves wash the sand,
and fresh water meets salt water.

The sea birds are calling.

The sea winds are blowing.

The journey is over.

All rivers have a beginning . . .

Trace the river from start to finish and discover some new river words along the way.

upriver (toward the source)

The beginning of a river is called its **source**. Some rivers start with melting snow and ice. Others begin with a spring bubbling up from under the ground.

A stream that joins another stream or river is called a **tributary**.

A fast-moving river carries along lots of pebbles and soil, and these rub against the riverbed like sandpaper, slowly wearing it away. This "wearing away" of the land is called **erosion**.

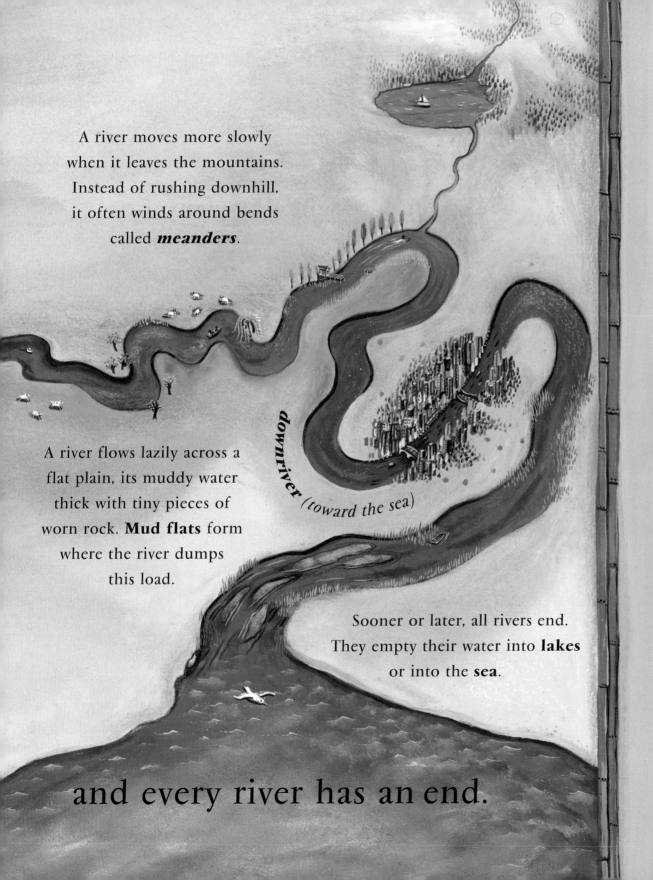

A river moves more slowly when it leaves the mountains. Instead of rushing downhill, it often winds around bends called **meanders**.

A river flows lazily across a flat plain, its muddy water thick with tiny pieces of worn rock. **Mud flats** form where the river dumps this load.

downriver (toward the sea)

Sooner or later, all rivers end. They empty their water into **lakes** or into the **sea**.

and every river has an end.

Look up the pages to find out about all these river things.

About the author

Meredith Hooper has written many books for children, including *Who Built the Pyramid?* She says the river in *River Story* is partly based on one that flowed past her garden, but that it mostly reflects "the strong-flowing big rivers of America, the fast, turbulent rivers of the Swiss Alps, the wide city rivers of Europe, and the meetings of river and sea that happen all over the world. Because as well as writing books, I like to travel!"

About the illustrator

Bee Willey is the illustrator of *Michael Rosen's ABC* and several collections of myths and legends. She says, "The rhythms inside *River Story*—water appearing at the source, trickling, gaining speed, and collecting things till it finally reaches the sea—paralleled the flow of teamwork that went into making the book. We had visions, memories, and information that we had to pull together, sometimes hitting rocky impasses and diversions, but finally flowing freely. It is one of those books that has really forged its own life, which I hope will translate to the readers."

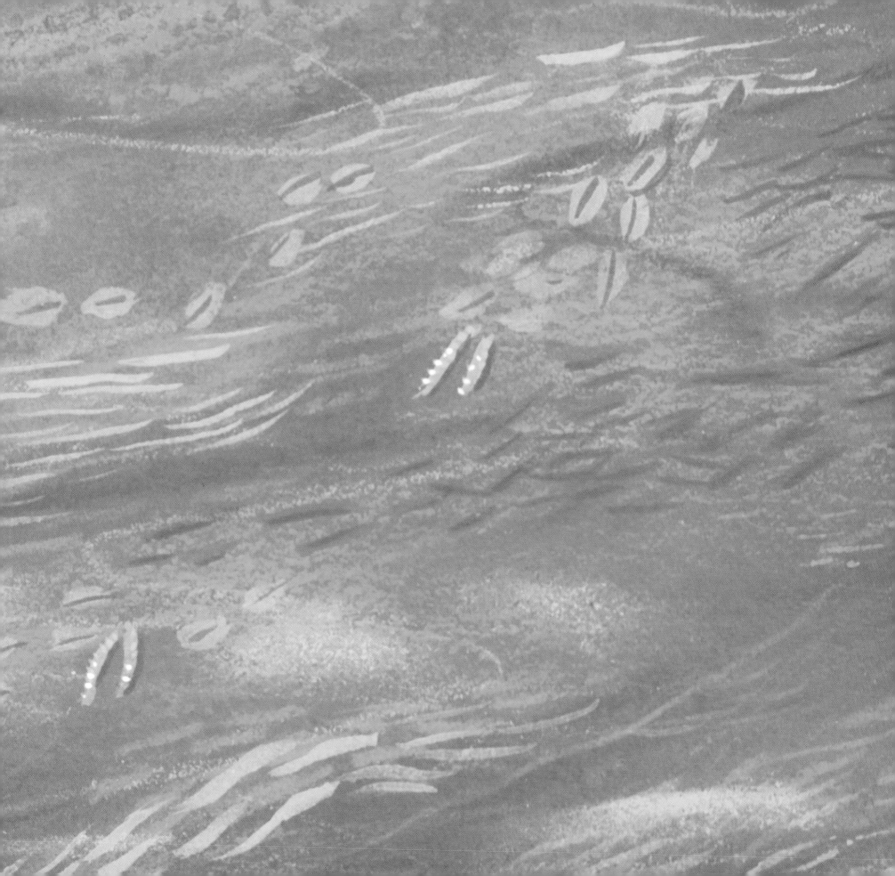